RACIST P.I.G.'S

How Progressive Identity Groups are Dividing America

by Andrew Coulter
copyright 2015

"I look to a day when people will not be judged by the color of their skin, but by the content of their character." - Martin Luther King, Jr

Contents

Afterword

1. Racial-Fascism in Obamaville

The relentlessness with which the Progressive Democrats have attacked our southern border has nothing to do with humanitarianism and everything to do with the acquisition of political power. In contrast to Conservative Republicans, who believe in property rights and national security, the Progressive Democrats have consistently attacked private property rights on every level, from confiscatory taxation to their stated intention of disarming the general public.

What every totalitarian understands is that no individual rights are possible and no political freedom is guaranteed to the disarmed citizen. Under the mantle of reducing violence, the Progressives and their state controlled media cohorts are advancing a totalitarian form of government.The Progressives want us unarmed for the same reason that Southern plantation owners wanted their slaves disarmed. They want us defenseless because they want our property, up to, and including our bodies. In other words, they want to reduce us to serfs, or slaves. And what is a slave but an individual deprived of property rights?

All rights are predicated upon the edifice of property rights, which includes the ownership of one's own body and mind. The Progressive attacks on free speech may be cloaked in good intentions, such as that of eliminating "hate", but in practice, political correctness is too subjective and too selective in its application to be anything other than what it is: statist thought policing. The Progressivism is just a euphemism for fascism but it sounds nice because it contains the word "progress," much like Liberalism sounds nice because it contains the word "liberal." Like all totalitarians, Progressives redefine words in order to deceive and control the masses.

To all those who are shaking their heads, confused as to why I put the blame on the Progressives, let me explain why this is so, for I am not a partisan and I have no agenda of my own. The Progressives are ideologically closer to socialism than capitalism, and socialism is by definition the gradual elimination of personal wealth through state directed redistribution. They seek to "ration" everything until a balance is achieved, a utopian enterprise to say in the least but one which, as history attests, actually leads to an equality of poverty. Socialism, whenever it is tried, levels the society by plundering and expropriating the middle class, resulting in a permanent underclass and an elite upper class. The middle class is replaced with an army of police who do the bidding of the elite at the top of the pyramid.

The elitists have decided that the best way to destroy America is no more complicated than a two-headed Trojan Horse: the DREAMer's are actually "sleeper agents"---the mass importation of "children" from third world nations represent, as Obama put it, the future upon which "our nation rests." Well, it's true. America will rest---in pieces----if the plan is fully implemented.

The plan is utopian and totalitarian, and has many facets and strategies at its disposal, for instance, the Cloward and Piven Strategy, which calls for the mass immigration for the purpose of overloading the welfare and social services. Then there is The Plan of San Diego, an old one which has been improved upon and given a new rationale, that involves an insurrection of immigrants who will be used as front line soldiers against a divided nation, serving the ends of the statist, anti-capitalist Left. The Democrats, the once and future party of slavery, under the Anti-Lincoln, will make the Constitution, which was written for freedom loving people, obsolete.

It's simple: they will overload the welfare system with their imported voter base, creating a massive number of government dependents who have no vested interest in free enterprise or its preservation. These will be the soldiers in the coming civil war which will put the Progressives against Conservatives. The Libertarians will mostly side with Progressives because they too have been duped into fearing Corporate America more than concentrations of state power.

The Plan of San Diego calls for the interment or extermination the white population, and the enslavement of boys and girls of sixteen years of age and younger. This Plan was originally conceived as a way for Mexico to "reclaim" the lands "stolen" by Europeans. It was an explicitly racist plan. The Weathermen Underground have improved it in the sense that now the genocide will be against "white capitalists," which was a smart addendum considering that most Progressives are white liberals, albeit self-hating whites who are massively ashamed of their "whiteness".

The "reconquest" of America will be accomplished by hordes of ignorant and illiterate people who are being inculcated with ideas which conflict with the American dream. Instead of rugged individualism and entrepreneurialism, they are imported as refugees who are indirect victims of America's success and therefore entitled to reparations. The sinister Progressives have used racial identity movements to psychologically segregate society more totally than it was under Jim Crow.

The Progressive lies are rooted in a false dichotomy which labels whites as privileged, and non-whites as oppressed. All non-whites are being herded into categories and told to stand in solidarity against the whites. For example, the blacks are being called upon to answer to their racial pride and ancestral grievances, and the black pride movements unanimously call for the subjugation and annihilation of the "white devils" and the Jews, who comprise the evil one percent that oppress the masses of "colored" people.

The "La Raza" movement was created by a Nazi propagandist named Jose Consuelos. This Nazi invented the myth of Aztlan and the "Cosmic Race" and published "La Raza Cosmica" the same year that "Mein Kampf" was released, and for the same purposes. Each called for a reclaiming of an ancient homeland, extolling the virtues of "blood and soil," and both believed that utopia could be achieved with racial solidarity and totalitarianism. To the Nazi's, the ethnic cleansing of Germany was a social justice crusade. The Nazi's were radical leftists, vegetarians, proto-hippies, and Progressives. They believed that one percent of the population was exploiting the rest and that it would be moral spread their wealth around.

The Nazi ideology has found new expression in the Occupy Wall Street movement, Anonymous, Environmentalism, New Ageism, and in Social Justice cults everywhere. Much of Jose Consuelos' writings were awash with New Age nonsense about "Atlantis" and "Lemuria." (The Lemurians, it should be pointed out, were the original Africans, according to Consuelos. Lemurians were the race that existed before Atlanteans, and by all accounts were mentally underdeveloped, egg-laying hermaphrodites that sexually abused animals.)

"Whiteness" is the new "Jewishness" and it is viewed by Progressive academicians as a social construct that must be eliminated if "equality" is to be achieved. If the Progressives succeed, then the coming civil war and the genocide that follows will be barbaric and evil beyond imagining. It will be awful, and the rest of the world will watch and cheer. No one will help because the world is largely anti-capitalist now and the greed of the communists, the socialists, and the fascists from all over the world want their fair share of the American Pie. They truly desire a Social Justice Holocaust. Even the Vatican will side with the racist, fascist mobs---just as they publicly supported Hitler in his time. The Muslim Brotherhood too, will cheer the bloodletting--just as they too, praised the Nazis.

The Progressives are brainwashed, egocentric, ethnocentric, and ideologically bigoted collectivists, traitors to their own souls. They must be stopped in their well-intentioned crusade for "equality" before they regress back to the darkest days of the Twentieth Century. We must each, as individuals, stand up against the Progressive Identity Groups (the PIGs), and fight for our nation, our values, and our freedoms, or we shall lose them by default. The American Dream will turn into a grotesque, un-American Nightmare.

2. Check the Box: Racialism and Identity Politics

"You white, Private. You is white."

Staff Sergeant Jones repeated it like a mantra and yet, I steadfastly refused to check any of the boxes. To check a box on race, in any context, is to accept the premise of racialism. I rejected racialism at a young age. Racial pride never appealed to me. It was not an easy stand to take in the US Army, which requires individuals to relinquish their individuality. Race, in that context, was just another detail in the endless classifications, categorizations, and assessments each soldier is besieged with. In this particular instance, my refusal to choose a race was delaying the entire platoon, most of whom were self-identified "blacks". A couple "Hispanics," and "Asian", and a handful of "whites" stood at parade rest, anxious to go home, angrily awaiting my capitulation.

The blacks, the white, and the Asian agreed that I was white, while the Hispanics claimed me as one of their own. To check off on any race, I felt, was to renounce my individuality in lieu of group identity on the basis of something I have no control over. I didn't want be branded, didn't want to dignify their stupid census. I refused to select a race. Instead, I explained that my reticence to group myself according to the superficialities of phenotypic differences was predicated upon my firm belief in the primacy of the content of one's character more so than the color of one's skin....
There I was being coerced into choosing a tribe in order to complete some tedious intra-company census.

I suppose it was my height, or rather my lack of it, which led me to understand at an early age how group psychology tends to focus its caprice upon the non-conformist. As a short person. I was treated vastly better than the obese in most instances. What the obese and the short have in common is that we are outside of the collective comfort zone known as "The Average." Average is a safe place to be. It means that one's uniqueness blends into an indistinct crowd of averageness, lessening the chance of being singled out.

I, however, am not interested in averaging myself out. Racial consciousness is self-betrayal and a source of false, unearned pride. I am beyond that shallow form of ethnocentrism. I am post-racial and this makes me an outsider. Outsiders are always feared, hated, ridiculed, or respected, depending upon what it is that sets them apart from the rest.

Of all collectives, racial collectives are the most acutely aware of inter-group differences. Their very existence is based upon maintaining the group's purity, its monochromatic homogeneity, . The central irony of racialism is that a racial collective only exists in relation to other racial collectives, and each racial group holds itself as superior to all the others. Black supremacists view whites as devils and vice versa; Arab supremacists see other races as apes and pigs, and the white supremacists have invented eugenics to grant themselves a pseudo-scientific rationale for their hateful ideology. Despite their superficial differences, the bigotry of racists around the world is the same, and in homogeneous societies, other differences are capitalized upon, i.e. tribal warfare within racial groups. Racial collectivism is just one denomination of Groupthink, which is how all P.I.G.'s think.

Groupthink is an atavistic, pre-rational, emotion driven operating system. When individuals within a mob or religious cult are communicating and interacting as a collective they operate as cells within a larger organism. Groupthink is a catalyst for organizing and agitating community action, but while there is strength in numbers, numbers don't guarantee clearer thinking or better ideas. Numbers merely provide the labor to enact bad ideas. This is consistent with the collectivists emphasis on "people power" over individual initiative.

Individuality and the novelties it brings forth are ridiculed, worshipped, or treated with hostility by collectivists whenever they gather in large enough numbers. A group of collectivists becomes a self-reinforcing echo chamber, and the separate constituents merge their identities into that super-beast, the mob. Mobs provide shelter, security, identity, and power for those willing to merge their own interests with that of their mob. To abandon or be kicked out of a group is to be left to fend for oneself, to lose group protection and group identity. Such is the tough love of the gang, the cult, and any other form of collectivist tribe; they love you, so long as you conform to peer pressure.

Collectivist love, however, is ultimately a conditional love. When those conditions are violated the love is retracted. This is why those who choose to renounce their racial affiliation and be recognized for individual achievements are denounced by the groups they reject. Race is a tool. It's a means to an end for the statist, which explains why the National Association for the Advancement of Colored People will not allow black Conservatives to speak at their conventions. They aren't about advancing individuals, individualism, or the economic system of capitalism, which is driven by individuals seeking to accrue personal wealth.The NAACP. or the NAALCP as Rush Limbaugh calls it (L is for Liberal), is a Progressive Identity Group, a race P.I.G., and P.I.G.'s are about one thing and one thing only: Power.

Hell hath no fury like an identity politics group scorned, as attested by the "self-hating" gays, by "race-traitor's", "Uncle Toms," "coconuts", "apostates," and every other variant of free thinker seeking freedom from the intimidation of group coercion. Take Bruce Jenner, for example. He was lauded as an icon for his courage in "coming out" as a transexual, but was later revilled for also coming out as a Republican. For the Progressive Identity Groups, the only thing worse than a Republican or Conservative is one with a legitimate claim to minority-group status. These apostates have their characters assassinated in a very public way. It is this ability to out-group and destroy the non-conformist that is the P.I.G.'s hidden source of power.

Sometimes, however, even race isn't enough: Governor Bill Richardson deemed Senator Ted Cruz an "inauthentic Hispanic" while Barack Obama is given a pass on blackness despite having a white mother and an upbringing among liberals, communists, and rich white people. George Zimmerman, the night-watchmen who inadvertently provoked a fight with a teenager resulting in the teen being shot and fatally wounded, was categorized by the media as a "White-Hispanic", a racial category invented on the spot in order to justify the white on black hate crime narrative the Progressive media was promulgating. This conflicted with Zimmerman's dark skin, dark eyes, and what might best be described as South American facial features.

Racialism is the most basic and primitive form of collectivism. It places primary importance on the most obvious surface characteristics of the individual in order to filter the person according to those who have an approximate skin color match. The content of the character is of no importance to the racial collectivist, except as secondary characteristics which are only accepted as valid if they serve the interests of the race.

Republics safeguard individual liberty against consensus tyranny and the oppression of majority rule. The Democrat Party, by contrast is a vehicle for collectivism in the form of Unionism, Feminism, Racialism, and every other kind of Identity Politics. Individuals have no place in their collectivized, group-think approach to politics, and so any individuals who fail to report to their respective group are traitors to their group. Modern Democrats are more Lenin than Madison when it comes to their interpretation of democracy.

Fascism, totalitarianism, authoritarianism, are all systems designed for ruling over collectives, or classes, or castes, or slaves, or prisoners. Collectivism is antithetical to the individual seeking self-determination, i,e, the pursuit of happiness. Black Power, Brown Power, White Power, Gay Power, Girl Power, and other forms of "people power" claim to stand up for whichever "minority" they proclaim to represent, but in the process they overlook the smallest minority of all, which is and always will be, the individual.

Racialism is a tool for oppression and the hypocrisy of those who use it as such is laid bare for all to see. This insight, however, can only be had by those who can look past their own skin color, identity cult, and personal prejudices. Notice, for instance, how those who support affirmative action tend to oppose racial profiling. That level of selectivity in the application of race-conscious policy belies bias, bigotry, and covert racism (which today is most often the acceptable racism against whites). Notice how accusations of "racism" are flung at those who are politically opposed to Democrat policies. Such accusations are used to stifle debate and to impose limits on free speech. Notice too how "white right-wingers" are demonized by the Mainstream Media, which is a the public relations arm of the Democrat Party.A truly objective media would call out the Progressives on their disingenuous tactics.

"White Privilege" is just another racialist contrivance designed to cause lighter skinned people to self-identify as oppressors and to feel really, really bad about it. White Privilege is a tool with which Progressive Whites can renounce their own "whiteness" by owning up to their "inherent" racism, and admit that they unfairly benefit from a society based upon white privilege. By accepting White Guilt, the white Progressives can atone for the sins of the past. At the Occupy Wall Street protests, for example, white males were not allowed to use the megaphones to address the amassed crowds until all "oppressed minorities" and women had their say first. Many white individuals now wear white wristbands as a reminder to "check their privilege." In other words, they are not allowed to just be themselves--they are now racially collectivized and responsible for the actions of their ancestors, who may or may not have been slave-owners---and in all likelihood are descended from slaves themselves.

Eventually, out of respect for the others in my squad, I chose a race. I selected the blank spot reserved for "other" and filled the blank with Chinese-Black-Samoan-Jew. That small rebellious act left an indelible imprint on my world-view. It stunned me just how easily people could see themselves and others as being differentiated by skin color rather than merit; how easily people have forgotten the message of Martin Luther King Jr.; and how distant now that dream he had of a post-racial society.

3. Be Wise as Latinas

I was raised in an ethnocentric, race conscious family. There was a certain degree of racial pride but no overt signs of racism. Besides, racism was something white people did. Racial enmity was something seen on television, read about in the papers, and written about in textbooks. It involved violence, terrorism, and oppression. It was about power, hatred, xenophobia, and fear. Racists were terrible people: loud, bossy, arrogant, and prideful. They were Klansmen, Skinheads, and backward hillbillies inhabiting the wilderness between the West and East coasts. Oh yeah, and only white people could be considered racist. All others, including my own hispanic family, that exhibiting racism were merely engaging in "reverse racism", which isn't really racism because the "oppressed" don't have power over others. Racism, as is popularly understood in America today, is something one does, not just a world-view. Or so I was told.

What I was exposed to in real life, however, was racialism in the form of ethnocentrism, and in our case, a form of cultural vanity. I was raised with multicultural awareness, a bit of pride in "our heritage", and a celebration of diversity. There was nothing wrong about it I supposed. My family was one which embraced the idea of La Raza, the idea of a new nation, a race created by a divinely ordained merging of the descendants of the Spanish and the indigenous populations of North America. We were the La Raza Cosmica, the Cosmic Race.Instead of having pride in our individuality, we were expected to be prideful as exemplars of our particular ethnic enclave.

We were Chicanos privately, Latino publicly, and Hispanic according to the boxes we checked on whatever forms we were required to fill out. The way I understood it, "whiteness" was a generic culture with a long history of oppressing other races. Whites were awkward, culture-less, bland, and incapable of dancing or of looking cool. Whites were seen as nerds, dorks, and ineffectual weaklings who occupied a moral low-ground because of their historical oppression of the other races. As Chicanos, my family consciously identified with the indigenous Mexican blood in our otherwise white looking bodies. Our ancestors were Spanish but we chose the designation Chicanos, and we culturally sided against whiteness.

I wasn't drawn into it by choice. I was born into it and I grew to reject it. Religion, race, and team sports never appealed to me. I was born an outsider. What made racialism so obnoxious to me as a teenager was its negation of individual character. I could reject or accept any philosophy, ideology, and mode of personal expression. No avenue was closed to me. I could become whatever I wanted to. Yet, I was still expected to be a representative of what the collective wished to see. There's a lot of peer pressure in racial pride groups. It has a very cult-like aspect to it which I resented. I didn't like the idea that I belonged to a group because of geographic and genetic affinity rather than conscious choice.. My older sisters and younger brothers were all majoring in Chicano Studies at the university. I flipped through one of those textbooks once and noticed a bit of graffiti on the inside cover: Old English font spelled out BROWN PRIDE. How can one take pride in something not earned? BROWN POMP would have made more sense to me.

My family attended a Hispanic conferences of one kind of another on a regular basis. We went to Hispanic job fairs, subscribed to Hispanic newsletters, attended Hispanic art exhibits, and went to Catholic Mass conducted in Spanish. And yet, it all went over my head. Race was boring to me. It was an outmoded concept. Despite being surrounded by the ideas of "The People," of Che Guevara, and "La Raza"; despite all those subtle jabs at "Gringos", it did not occur to me that my family held deeply racist views. They weren't explicit about it. However, it eventually dawned on me that the entire concept of Hispanic, or Chicano, and Latino, were all social constructs that encouraged people with darker skin to self-segregate. I was witnessing, first hand, the flowering of a nationalist movement based upon racial solidarity and a barely disguised antipathy towards white people and "whiteness"

In college I avoided ethnic studies and instead majored in journalism because I wanted to learn to write news commentary. I dropped out in the first semester after being annoyed by the racial politics within the journalism department itself. There was racialism, sexism, Marxism, and anti-Republicanism in every lecture. The textbook was all but ignored and instead we had meandering group discussions about news of the day and our opinions were solicited. The discussions went nowhere; the least informed were given equal time and credibility as everyone else and the conversations tended towards generalized statements about the oppressors: rich white Republicans.

I was invited by a professor to attend a Women in Journalism conference. She was an avowed Marxist and liked to mention the fact that her vehicle was an old beat up Volkswagen, and how she could have more money if she wanted to sell out to

Corporate America, but instead she was there with us, doing her best to summarize Howard Zinn's A People's History of the United States. Her delivery was intended to entertain and elicit laughter, not to invite questions or comments. She smacked her gums to affect a cool nonchalance. I wanted to learn to write news commentary and was instead subjected to Leftist ideological subversion. Worst of all, nobody seemed to care.

My professor and I were talking about the recent appointment of Sonia Sotomayor to the Supreme Court when I pressed her for an opinion regarding Sotomayor's statement that a "wise Latina" would be a better judge than a white man with similar qualifications. I was baffled by her response: "Yes, we need more women in positions of power, and certainly a minority will have a richer tapestry of life experiences to draw from than a white person who is coming from a place of privilege."

I thought it was sad that she was so obsessed with her sexism, her victim-politics, her group-think, and her blatant racialism. I was barely twenty and she was in her fifties. I couldn't imagine being that deceived for so long. What could be more tragic than to be sentenced to a lifetime of narrow-mindedness and bigotry and not even know it?

I withdrew from school and started blogging. To make ends meet, I sold halloween costumes and masks through an online auction until another "wise Latina" shut my store down. I was selling the most popular costume at that time--a space alien with an orange jumpsuit and a green card. It was called "The Illegal Alien" and I was selling out as fast as I could list them. Then, as soon as it had begun, the flow of sales was dammed when a La Raza activist reported the item as racially offensive. She was interviewed on a website called "Red, Brown, and Blue," maintained by a La Raza member who envisions an America without white people.

The orders for the "offensive" costumes were refunded and my store was suspended. It was then that I realized that the double-standards and logical inconsistencies I once found humorous now had the power to affect my income. Racialist Progressive Identity Groups, or Race P.I.G.'s as I have come to know them, had declared war upon me and my free-thinking way of life. Had I embraced racialism instead of radical individualism, perhaps I would have been offended by that costume as well.

Collectivists, it can be observed, not only believe in collective guilt but in collective pain, collective anger, and collective sadness. If something is offensive to the group, the race, or the religion, all of its adherents are obliged to feel offended. Supposedly, positive attributes are also collectively shared, thus, a Latina is inherently wiser than a white male. The more Progressive Identity Groups one belongs to, the greater one's virtue. Therefore, a woman from an "oppressed" minority is more virtuous than a "privileged" male. If you throw in a sexual proclivity which differs from the norm or perhaps the victim bona fides of a mass shooting incident survivor, then you have a candidate for public office.

All P.I.G.'s are aggrieved martyr cults at the core. Every Progressive Identity Group has an innocent victim and a guilty devil. According to the Progressive faith, the more one has suffered, the greater the virtue one accrues. Conversely, the more successful one is, the greater one's evil. All rich CEO's are evil and all poor people are angels. White men exist at the bottom of the Progressive's morality scale. Illegal immigrant transvestites rate near the top. while blacks and latino's must compete for the middle area above the Asians, who sit astride the whites. A "wise Latina" trumps a white man in every field of endeavor according to the Progressives because they emphasize form over substance, image over ability, and skin color over character.

4. The Klan with a Tan

The Republican Party emerged in 1854 as the anti-slavery party to combat the Kansas Nebraska Act, which threatened to extend slavery into those territories; they aimed instead to promote modernization of the South's economy. After the Civil War, the Republican-dominated Congress forced a Radical Reconstruction policy on the South, which saw the passage of the 13th, 14th, and 15th amendments to the Constitution, and the granting of equal rights to all Southern citizens. All three of these amendments were fought against by the Democrats.

The KKK was founded by Southern Democrats after the Civil War. Their intention was to maintain their hold on black labor by any means necessary. This included terrorism, intimidation, violence, and the deliberate fostering of racial animosity. Laws were passed to prevent blacks from owning guns because it's difficult to enslave or lynch an armed man. These were the first gun laws in the nation and they were specifically intended to keep blacks from having any real political power. Additionally, laws were passed barring blacks from hunting, fishing, or attending school--laws which criminalized self-sufficiency and made it impossible for blacks to engage in free enterprise, to chase the American Dream. The Democrat Party has always aimed to put an end to self-sufficiency itself, after all, slaves must be dependent upon their masters if they are to be of any service.

It's not a coincidence that the Democrat party opposed the civil rights acts, nor should it be a mystery as to which political party opposes gun ownership by private citizens today. It should also be pointed out that, despite modern day Democrats calling the National Rifle Association "Klansmen", the N.R.A. has, in fact, a history of chartering groups specifically for blacks so they could defend themselves against the KKK.

It's also noteworthy that the KKK were great supporters of Margaret Sanger, the founder of Planned Parenthood. They were in agreement about what they mutually decried as "The Negro Problem," and saw a solution in population reduction by sterilization, contraception, and abortion. The Ku Klux Klan was the terrorist wing of the Democrat Party and it demonstrably harbors genocidal ambitions against black people. It's shocking but true.

The duplicity of the Democrat Party with regards to racialism is laid bare in its endorsement of the National Council on La Raza. In July of 2014, President Obama signaled something portentous, if not alarming with regards to La Raza's brand of racialism. He attended a fundraising event at the Texas home of Robert Rodriguez, one of the leaders of the La Raza movement. His conspicuous presence there highlighted his equally conspicuous absence from the south Texas border, which had just seen an escalation in the already massive influx of illegal immigrants.

This influx was both something the President and his administration organized, yet they refused to publicly acknowledge as a problem. The fact that violent gang members, terrorists, and drug mules are a part of the influx is seemingly of no concern to the supporters of the invasion. This invasion, and that is what it is, happens to fit nicely within La Raza's racial mythos, in which America is actually Aztlan, the long lost homeland of the "Cosmic Race," who are the true owners of the land and whose destiny it is to occupy it as a "Bronze nation." In their view, America is the oppressor and they, as La Raza, are entitled to reparations in the form of the land we presently know as California, Nevada, Arizona, Colorado, and New Mexico.

Robert Rodriguez is not just a director and a leader in a powerful racial lobby; he's the director of the most egregiously racist film since Birth of a Nation. Birth of a Nation, based on a novel entitled The Klansman, was a call to arms propaganda film which presented the Ku Klux Klan as the heroic defenders of the homeland against the newly freed blacks. Blacks were played by white men in blackface who caricatured blacks as barbarous, dumb, lazy, and crude towards women---the way the Progressives characterize white men today. The movie posters for the film depict a proud Klansman holding a burning torch.

Robert Rodriguez's film Machete is a call to arms propaganda film which presents La Raza as the heroes, righteously taking up arms against the white oppressors. Whites are depicted as crude, barbarous, incestuous, drug addled, gun-toting psychopaths. The movie presents La Raza as taking back what is rightfully theirs. As the wise Latina heroine puts it, "We didn't cross the border! The border crossed us!" The movie poster for Machete depicts a Mexican warrior with a machete held aloft, standing before a burning Capitol Dome in the background. His pose and the composition of the poster itself is, when examined side by side, the same as Birth of a Nation's movie poster, only with a different racial champion.

In Machete, Lindsay Lohan is presented as a typical American white woman: a drunken slut with no skills and loose morals. The heroine of the story, played by Jessica Alba, is a healer, a warrior, and a virtuous Latina. This dynamic is mirrored by the character Machete, a righteous, self-effacing warrior pitted against slovenly border patrol agents who delight in murdering pregnant illegal immigrants, or "cockroaches" as the two-dimensional caricatures describe them in Rodriguez's racial agitprop. The film's climactic race war is abetted by the Catholic Church, which is interesting considering the Catholic Church's active role in facilitating the border crisis.

Just what was it that Rodriguez, a veritable Joseph Goebbels of the La Raza movement discussed with President Obama? Perhaps they were talking about Obama's Latino credentials, for Obama is a de-facto adoptee into La Raza by Geraldo Rivera who, at a National Council of La Raza meeting, declared that Obama is "one of us," meaning a latino. Ironically, Geraldo Rivera happens to be Jewish, but he changed his name from Jerry Rivers to Geraldo Rivera in order to ingratiate himself to La Raza. This makes him transracial and apparently gives him the authority to declare Obama transracial as well, although the trend today is for racialists to claim "bi-racial" status as a way of double dipping into the race racket. Even George Lopez, the virulently racist comedian and anti-white bigot, has also granted President Obama his Latino credentials, declaring him "very Latino." The fact is, if Barack Obama was a Republican, he'd be considered an "inauthentic black" and it would be pointed out that he doesn't have real "slave blood." His skin color would actually work against him for there's no group more reviled by the Progressives than racial apostates.

More likely, Robert Rodriguez and President Obama were discussing the funding for the next instalment in the Machete franchise, this time, perhaps a MACHETE: Fast and Furious, where a bunch of La Raza supremacists mow down Americans with the M16's supplied by Eric J Holder. Perhaps Obama could make a cameo as a police officer setting dogs loose on Tea Party members while Al Sharpton and Jesse Jackson man the fire hose. Such a film would be only slightly more blatant than MACHETE, or as I like to call it, Afterbirth of a Nation.

5. Genocidal P.I.G.'s

"It's why Obama is elected now. He is the first, I maintain, Latino president. He's the first brown president. Why? He could be, and he looks Puerto Rican. And the point is, he would not be president but for the Latino vote and the Latino vote was, for the first time in my lifetime, an expression of a community understanding its responsibilities..." --- Geraldo Rivera addressing the National Council of La Raza, 2008

This line of thinking is aligned with Jose Consuelo's race obsessed manifesto La Raza Cosmica in which he mused that blacks would "merge" with the other races and thereby be "redeemed":

"...The lower types of the species will be absorbed by the superior type. In this manner, for example, the Black could be redeemed, and step by step, by voluntary extinction, the uglier stocks will give way to the more handsome. By grafting on to the related race, Blacks would take the jump of millions of years that separate Atlantis from our times, and in a few decades of aesthetic eugenics, the Black my disappear, together with the types that a free instinct of beauty will recognize as undeserving of perpetuation."-- Jose Consuelo, La Raza Cósmica

This is especially sinister when considering how the eugenicist Margaret Sanger, founder of Planned Parenthood, discussed the need to coerce the blacks into self-extermination through voluntary abortion. Planned Parenthood has a sordid history of targeting black communities, perpetuation what many describe as "womb lynching," with blacks accounting for 50% of all abortions in the United States despite only comprising 13% of the total population.

Margaret Sanger, for whom the Margaret Sanger Award is named, was a darling of the Ku Klux Klan and was admired by Adolf Hitler himself. "I accepted an invitation to talk to the women's branch of the Ku Klux Klan...I saw through the door dim figures parading with banners and illuminated crosses...I was escorted to the platform, was introduced, and began to speak...In the end, through simple illustrations I believed I had accomplished my purpose. A dozen invitations to speak to similar groups were proffered." (Margaret Sanger: An Autobiography, P.366)

Sanger became a "birth control martyr" when she was arrested for handing out condoms in 1917. By using victim politics, she was able to convince women of "inferior races" to self-exterminate. "We do not want word to go out," she wrote to a colleague, "that we want to exterminate the Negro population, and the minister is the man who can straighten out that idea if it ever occurs to any of their more rebellious members." In the Progressive faith, Sanger is a saint, a martyr, and a Feminist icon. Not surprisingly, Hillary Clinton is among the proud recipients of the Margaret Sanger Award.

Feminism is anti-nuclear family and Progressivism is white supremacist at its rotten core; Sanger united these two elements of the political left, birthing an advanced, covert eugenics operation which makes Nazi racial hygiene look tame by comparison, quantitatively speaking, considering the more than fifty million abortions since Roe v. Wade in 1973. Qualitatively, there might be a comparison, but first it would have to be established that the unborn can feel pain and experience the horror of their own deaths.

What Geraldo Rivera revealed by pandering to La Raza was the manner in which all Racial P.I.G.'s see other races and ,moreover, just how shallow their character assessments are. Progressive Identity Groups cannot see past race, creed, or political affiliation. They are fundamentally class-conscious. To them, the individual is invisible, immaterial, and non-existent. They see only things, objects, and animals. What makes us human, I believe,, is not our skin color but our individuality, our souls. Progressives are soulless. They sell their souls in exchange for the benefits of tribal association. This isn't inherently bad; Identity Groups are an important fixture in all human societies, across all cultures and throughout all of history. Progressive Identity Groups are different in that they mask ulterior motives; they are fraudulent and soulless, cynically engineered and puppeteered by demagogues for the purpose of opposing individuality.

America is a nation founded upon the principle of individual liberty, therefore, it only makes sense that the P.I.G.'s of all variety begin with the premise that America needs to be fundamentally transformed. P.I.G.'s aim to replace individual liberty with collective bondage and will stop at nothing to get their way. Today's Progressive Democrats, like the slave owning Democrats of the past, require a permanent underclass to rule over, and thanks to the scourge of identity politics, they have managed to win back many the descendants of those they once enslaved. A Brave New World is emerging: a world of happy slaves and powerful overlords.

6. High Horse Sh*t

The Progressives smear their enemies with manure in order to make themselves look better by comparison. This tactic is always directed towards putting America on the moral low ground. It's inculcated into the culture and language and, by default, the Progressives always assume the moral high ground in any debate.

This has been achieved by the use of Big Lies. Big Lies use false dichotomies and faulty premises, each constituting a tacit condemnation of Western values, the heart of which is individualism. Each Big Lie grants the believer another colored ribbon, another smug bumper sticker, and the right to look down their noses at those who don't believe same way. The conclusion inferred is that non-believers are either ignorant or evil.

There are relentless attempts to denigrate the achievements of Western civilization by citing some collective which has been harmed by it. The Progressives go to the extreme of excusing terrorists as "freedom fighters" while blaming capitalism for bad weather. Western values are blamed for the world's ills and the solutions proffered by the finger-pointers are always the same: more collectivism, more government programs, more taxation, and more regulation.

The ever divisive Progressives have introduced a simplistic yet effective false dichotomy separating the people of the world into the "99%" and the "1%". This was the Big Lie galvanizing the Occupy Wall Street protests. They believe that all "social inequality" results not from the reality that there are differences between individuals, but because a small minority has effectively monopolized all the resources, wealth, and opportunity. They don't blame individuals for individual failure just as they refuse to give credit to individuals for their own success. Obama pointed out that business owners are too impressed by their own efforts when their successes should be seen as a collective effort. "You didn't build that!" was his message to the entrepreneurs of America.

To the pessimistic Progressives, wealth is something which exists as a static supply, and thus, one man's gain is another man's loss. Life, they believe, is a zero sum game. To them, the concentration of private wealth necessitates that others go poor. Thus, the richest one percent are guilt of being rich. This view of capitalism gives a veneer of righteous indignation to the act of scapegoating the wealthy for the state of the poor. Nowhere in their arguments, however, is there any real discussion of the high standard of living enjoyed by America's "poor", or that the one percent may have "earned" it, or that not all poor are victims. This skewed perspective explains why tax cuts are looked at by Progressives as "loss of revenue." They see all wealth as evidence of theft and exploitation. They refuse to recognize that wealth in a free market is created by businesses meeting consumer needs, nor do they want to know that it only takes $30,000 per year to be in the top 1% of the world's richest population.

Pope Francis made public statements to the effect that the West is enjoying a "culture of waste," and that the food that a rich person throws away is the moral equivalent of taking food from the mouth of a starving person on the other side of the planet. This ridiculous idea makes sense only to those who have already accepted the Big Lie that life is a zero sum game. It is worth noting that Pope Francis' namesake Saint Francis, was a proto-environmentalist, an animal rights advocate, and a "humanitarian." What this translates to in practice is nature worship at the expense of denigrating man's "worldliness", elevating animals while rejecting man, and making ostentatious displays of compassion while renouncing wealth. The pope has chosen this association for these very reasons; Saint Francis sits astride the anti-wealth high horse, and since Pope Francis is a revolutionary Marxist, there could be no better association to have. Saint Francis lived the communist ideal: he quit a successful career and gave all his property and money to the poor so he could run around naked in the woods and talk to the animals, the moon, and the insects.

When examined objectively, poverty is not ennobling. Private wealth has elevated the standard of living of the world's poor more than all wealth redistribution of all the bleeding heart moral busybodies combined. With the fading influence of the Church as an opinion shaping mechanism for the state, the entertainment industry has filled in the gap. It has been promulgating the Big Lies of Progressivism under the guise of entertainment since its inception.

Consider the massively successful Avatar, in which the hero, a westerner who happens to be a marine, must renounce his race, his culture, and his nation in order to be accepted by the morally superior primitive society. Industrialism marked the end of collectivism stranglehold on upward mobility, and thus, industrialism is the devil and Capitalism is Satan's religion. Avatar's story is identical to that of Dances with Wolves, in which a soldier goes native, choosing the life of a "noble savage", siding with the original victims of "western imperialism". For all their talk about diversity, there is very little of it in Hollywood. Diversity and originality are both sacrificed to their ideology.

When Jihadi terrorists murder innocent Westerners, the Progressives excuse it as social justice, only they call it "blowback." This refers to their belief that Western values, such as freedom of speech, infuriates the rest of the world and blowback is what happens when those who don't share our values fight back. Collectivists don't look at the individuals committing the violence, but instead look at the aggrieved Political Identity Group the individuals belong to, and then examine it within the context of the Big Lie which posits that the free nations are enjoying freedom and wealth at the expense of the poorer, less free nations. Given that premise, all terrorist attacks against the United States are justifiable.

When the American Embassy in Benghazi was attacked on 9-11-2012, the blame for the terrorists' actions was placed squarely on America's freedom of speech. It was said by the US State Department, the President, and the state controlled media that our free speech has consequences and that we must learn to modify our use of it given the reality of modern communication. This view was uncontested by the collectivist left even when it was exposed as a blatant cover story--the real cause of the attack on the embassy having nothing to do with an obscure video on the Internet. It was uncontested because it fit within the worldview of the collectivists when it comes to their view of freedom: negative liberties are risky and positive liberties make society safe. Free speech is dangerous speech. Politically correct speech is safe. The politically correct today are treated with respect and their opinions are taken very seriously. Instead of laughing at the thought-police of today, people give them moral high ground, and society gets more high horse shit as a result.

Progressives are "social justice" advocates, and as such they view America as inherently racist and corrupt, down to its founding documents. To them, America was built on slavery, not in spite of it. Facts be damned, the Progressives will always believe the lies that fit within the confines of the Big Lie, and thus their bias makes them excellent apologists for any and all attacks against the freedoms which make the American Dream possible. Free individuals are dangerous to herd solidarity, and to the herd minded, capitalism is an evil system with evil roots because it leads to inequality of outcome.

The Progressives hate capitalism because precisely because they desire equality of outcomes rather than equality of opportunity. They want all people to succeed, which sounds noble enough, but it can only happen at the expense of the successful, and at the cost of regulating the freedom out of free enterprise.. They would rather have equality in misery than the inequality of results, even if it means limiting the success of the gifted, the lucky, the creative, and the ambitious. Their ideal is a utopian vision and it manifests itself by unjustly imposing anti-individual controls designed to give all "groups" equal representation. Merit has no place in their utopia. The Progressive utopia penalizes the successful, which is itself unjust, but they can be unjust and get away with it because they are presumed to have the moral high ground. Social Justice is Selective Justice.

Progressive group-think is polarizing; the group will always discourage treating outsiders as equals. Outsiders are ignorant or immoral judging by their refusal to accept the group's core beliefs. Just look how Progressives view those who don't believe in the "science" of global warming. To not believe in it is to be impugned as ignorant, crazy, dumb, brainwashed, or simply greedy and evil. However, science cannot be settled, for there will always be more data and it won't always fit the theory. Therefore, science isn't something to accept and believe as unalterable, unfalsifiable doctrine. Progressives believe in global warming because it gives them the moral high ground from which to criticize their political opponents. The fact that the world hasn't warmed in eighteen years doesn't matter because, to the Progressives, narratives always trump facts.

The false dichotomy between the haves and have-nots is based upon the false premise that wealth is a static quantity. The have-nots, in America at least, are the beneficiaries of the highest standard of living the world has ever known, and it is wealth derived from entrepreneurial capitalists. The self-described have-nots blame the haves for their own lack of productivity, even as they enjoy lives partly or wholly subsidized by the haves. Those who look around them and see a world divided into haves and have-nots are probably the greediest ingrates the world has ever known.

The myth of the "noble savage" has been applied to BUMS for far too long. Bums aren't inherently good. Homeless shelters are not brimming with do-gooders and kind-hearted victims of a capitalist society. Conversely, not all CEOs are plotting how to kill their customers and take over the world. The Progressive Mythos teaches that Republicans are rich and evil, while the Democrats represent "the little guy" and the minorities. To those with a sense of history, this is laughable, for the Democrat Party, the oldest political party, was pro-slavery, anti-civil rights, and opposed to women's suffrage.

It's laughable that so many Democrats fall for the propaganda because most of it is written to persuade children. Try this out on your Progressive friends: tell them that the average Republican senator has a net worth of nine million dollars. Listen to their responses, look at their mean faces, nodding in agreement that all Republicans are rich, evil bastards. After a moment goes by, mention that the average Democrat senator is worth eighteen million dollars. You will see the double-think taking place as they struggle to remain astride the Progressive high horse.

7. The American Palestinians

The Progressives see a parallel between the La Raza's goal of reconquering America and the struggle of the Palestinians against the state of Israel. Like all their false moral equivalencies, this one is rooted in two false premise. One is the presumption that the West is an imperialist power rooted in theft and exploitation. Second, it grants moral high ground to those it casts as underdogs. Thus, America and Israel are cast as oppressors while the Palestinians and the "Chicanos" are the oppressed.

According to this narrative, race and geography are intertwined, not unlike the "blood and soil" of the Nazi ideology, which emphasized blood and territory as granting specific people rights to the land they historically have occupied. Blood and soil ideologies idealize communal living and reject modernity in favor of "living off the land." The rejection of modernity manifests as anti-Capitalism, anti-Industrialism, and includes a rejection of Judeo-Christianity. The La Raza movements are vehemently anti-Semitic and are as opposed to Israel's existence as they are to America's. They view Israel and America as conquered lands by peoples' whose blood doesn't entitle them to it. La Raza demonstrators often demand that white Americans' "move back" to Europe.

Progressive Identity Groups are equally supportive of La Raza and Hamas despite the fact that the success of both would entail the destruction of Israel and America. P.I.G.'s, it must be understood, are united in their hatred for Western values. All Progressives Identity Groups, whether they are based on race, gender, the environment, or sexual orientation are anti-Israel for the same reason they are anti-America. It comes down to their narratives about oppressors and the oppressed, and these are nothing more than the Marxist view of "the rich versus the poor" recast along racial and ethnic lines. The Progressives found it necessary to reinvent their fundamental myths in the wake of economic Marxism's failure to unite the "workers of the world."

La Raza's latest ploy is to import poor children from south of Mexico to take advantage of laws intended to protect refugees. These children are cast as victims and used as human shields to stifle criticism of mass illegal immigration. What this narrative fails to mention is that children constitute only a fraction of the total number of illegal immigrants. The Progressive media ensures that the innocent children remain the face of illegal immigration, even though this means ignoring the tens of thousands of gang members, rapists, and criminals who have been set free on the streets of America.

The Progressive media also aids and abets the use of human shields in Palestine in order to keep Israel on the moral low ground. Those who oppose illegal immigration in America are said to hate immigrant children and those who support Israel's right to defend itself are branded as supporting the death of Palestinian children. This distortion is promulgated despite the known fact that children are literally used as human shields by the PLO when they use school houses as missile silos. They allow children to be killed for the photo opportunities and to advance their false narratives.

8. Elysium: The DREAMer's Promised Land

The movie Elysium, starring the pseudo-intellectual, joker-faced prostitute Matt Damon presented a dystopian future in which the evil white people moved into outer space in the ultimate act of "white flight," leaving the world below to suffer in poverty. This view is supported by the Progressive myth which contends that the poverty of the third-world is due to the wealth of the first-world nations. This is part of the zero-sum fallacy which underlies all of their fundamental beliefs and which goes a long way towards explains their misguided quest for "social equity." The film is a thinly disguised commercial for both Obamacare, and open borders. The white people (naturally), hoard the medical technology on their space station paradise and shoot missiles at anyone attempting to "illegally enter" Elysium.

Elysium means heaven, or paradise, which is especially telling because the myth of Aztlan, rooted in the racial myths of Jose Consuelos, posits that the white race, which was the fourth race to evolve according to La Raza doctrine, was required to develop the technologies which would then be seized by the fifth race, the Cosmic Raza. The concept of an earthly paradise (or one orbiting in the heavens), is a place where all one's needs are taken care of, so long as one is obedient. This is viewed by socialists, communists, and progressives as desirable. According to President Obama the Constitution is a "charter of negative liberties," because it doesn't authorize the government to provide for its citizens, but rather suggests how it must leave people alone, i.e. "free" from governmental coercion.

Progressives view freedom from government as a bad thing. They would prefer total government. Paradise to them, Hell to Conservatives, who eschew positive liberties as an encroachment on their personal freedom to take risk, to assume personal responsibility, and to advance beyond the sustenance provided by big government. Every prisoner is experiencing negative liberty, that is, their physical needs are provided for.

Poverty was the normal condition of the human race and this changed with the rise of the Industrial Revolution in the mid-eighteenth century. Through the benefits of modern science and technology the Western industrialized nations have made poverty an abnormal condition. It is easy to forget what a dramatic change this transformation has meant for the average person. In the United States, substantial progress has been made in the effort to reduce poverty to a residual level.

Warren Brookes, economic writer for the Boston Herald, has called attention to the fact that "In spite of spiraling inflation, and energy costs, socio-economic data now shows that less than 7 percent of all Americans live below the U.S. poverty line, and even this 7 percent live better than 85 percent of the rest of the world's population." While it may be true, as many Progressives like to point out, that the U.S uses over a third of the world's energy despite having only 6 percent of the world's population, Brookes points out that the critics usually fail to mention that the U.S. produces 40 percent of the world's food supply.

Despite America's achievements, the racial Progressive Identity Group (race P.I.G.) La Raza is still looking towards their racial utopia. Here is how one Dreamer expressed his vision of Elysium, or Aztlan as they know it:

MY VISION OF AZTLAN
by Nelli Temachtiani

After getting chewed out at work for like the fourth time and thinking about how messed up and dehumanizing this capitalistic system is, I was inspired to write about a free AZTLAN. This vision is what keeps me going, day by day. The idea that one day, the original inhabitants of these lands will rise up and reclaim their land again. In Aztlan, things will be different.

In Aztlan, everyone will own their home outright. No more bank notes. No more mortgages or property taxes. What you have is yours and you are free to do whatever you want with it as long as you respect your neighbors.

In Aztlan, everyone will have free health care. There will be no such thing as health insurance companies or monthly premiums to pay. If you need the care, you get it. All you have to do is sign your name on the dotted line and come right on in and meet many of our specially trained doctors. Its completely free.

In Aztlan, an education is open to anyone with an open mind and heart. Laptops will be provided for you along with supplies, books etc. Standards for passing will be rigorous and we will use a variety of learning techniques. If you don't understand the material, you take the course over again until you've mastered the subject. We won't put you on "academic probation." You learn at your own pace.

In Aztlan, you will hear music and poetry coming out of the mouths of our people and all people who reside here. Creative spaces where one can sing, dance, paint, and perform for others will be plentiful. Our forms of entertainment will be positive and based on love, peace, and artistic expression. We will laugh and be the healthiest we'd ever been.

In Aztlan, food is fresh, never processed. We will support organic farms and take steps to get rid of chemical pesticides and other activities that strip the earth of its health and food of its vital nutrients. We will learn how to grow our own food again and have stores at every corner, where one can obtain food for their families.

In Aztlan, both women and men will be respected for their strength, intelligence, generosity and heart. Not for their looks, their bank accounts or what kind of clothes they wear or cars they drive. Both shall receive a well rounded education.

In Aztlan, our jobs will be to help others grow We will go to work because we want to, not because we have to. We will create work that is fulfilling and meaningful. People in Aztlan will choose their work based on their talents, skills, and strengths. All work will be respected!

In Aztlan, if taxes are imposed, they will be fair and used for the good of the community.

In Aztlan, recreational activities will be plentiful and learning centers at every corner. Our political system will be a true democracy where everyone's voices are heard.

In Aztlan, the earth will be respected as a living and breathing organism. We will rid ourselves of our dependence on oil and nuclear energy, We will go green and build new infrastructure where modes of transportation will help everyone get to where they need to go. And you won't have to pay for car insurance anymore either!

In Aztlan, we will respect all people and all shall have what they need to survive. We will eradicate homelessness, poverty, WAR, and hopelessness. We will dismantle racism and become one chicano nation. In Aztlan, we will finally be free!!!!!!!!

At night, I close my eyes and remember the words of my ancestors who said we will one day rise up to reclaim this land again. Let us take heed and do everything we can to make our vision a reality. It won't be perfect, nothing is. But it will be a helluva a lot better than how we are living now. When reading about our history, I am always touched by the writers who said that our people would laugh sweetly and had the most remarkable health in the world. They wrote that our ancestors had gentle souls and shared what they had with others. Chicanos still have that same spirit today.

The only way to solve a community's problems is through self determination. That is, WE ARE IN THE DRIVERS SEAT. We determine our own destinies, not those who lord over us and exploit us at every turn. Aztlan can become a reality but first we must believe in it wholeheartedly and bring this vision to our communities. Are you ready to make Aztlan a reality?

(Reprinted without permission. Or should I say, undocumented permission?)

9. Permanent Underclass

Individuals are difficult to enslave when they're educated, armed, and informed. Authoritarians require dependent, ignorant, propertyless subjects in order to hold and maintain power.Imagine if every enslaved black on every Southern plantation had a rifle. It would have effectively put an end to the tortures and degradations inflicted by the Democrat slave-owners.

The opponents of private gun ownership today are the direct ideological descendants of the slave-owners. Gun-control itself was introduced by the former slave-owners after the Civil War in order to keep blacks unarmed. The newly freed blacks were not allowed to pack heat and not because they might accidentally shoot someone or commit a crime. The slaves were kept unarmed because freedom is attainable only to those who have the ability to own property, and property ownership is not possible to those who cannot defend it.

Now, obviously, not every person in a free country needs to be armed and prepared to defend their property. It's not feasible nor necessary. This is why the very limited role of government described in the Constitution included only three areas where government has legitimate purpose. Primary among these legitimate responsibilities is national defense. National defense includes defense from external enemy threats as well as internal criminal threats.

It is not a coincidence that the Progressive Democrats oppose national borders under the guise of caring for immigrant children and that they ostensibly oppose private gun ownership under the guise of caring for the public safety, especially that of "the children." Their attacks upon the nation's borders as well as the individual property rights are part of their strategic attack upon the capitalist system itself. By undermining national security and by promoting crime, which is what gun-control actually accomplishes, they undermine the ability of the individual to achieve financial success.

Civility itself is being undermined by those who seek to restrict the ability of individuals to prosper as independent, autonomous, free people. Just as the Ku Klux Klan stirred up racial animus between poor whites and poor blacks, their political, ideological, and philosophical heirs (today's Democrats) use the Main Stream Media to stir up interracial disharmony. Progressives would rather see black youth mobs flash robbing stores than working as cashiers. The minimum wage laws, originally conceived by Southern Democrats as a means to price blacks out of the labor market when it came to obtaining federal contracts, is still being used by Democrats and to the same end. Black unemployment is caused by the Progressive's war on the middle class, on free enterprise, and on upward mobility itself.

State power is lessened by individual freedom, and so the advocates of big government always seek to take away the ability of individuals to exist as such. They insist upon categorizing everyone into one Progressive Identity Group or another. They don't want individuals who happen to have dark skin engaging in commerce in a pluralistic multi-ethnic nation. They want "blacks" to vote as "blacks" to increase minimum wage because the "rich whites" are greedy.

Individualism is the philosophy holding that man is an end in himself, and exists as a sovereign entity. Collectivism holds that the individual is state property, an appendage of the whole. Wherever freedom has taken hold, the collectivist must work to undermine the individual's foothold, politically, economically, and intellectually. Thus, the relentless Progressive attacks on the individual's ability to hold property, to engage in voluntary exchange, and to think independently.

In the early 1990's, Hillary and Bill Clinton wanted to suppress the Internet for fear that a "people's media" would undermine the mainstream media, which the Democrats control. The deceptively titled "Net Neutrality" is another Democrat ploy to do to the Internet what they did to the airwaves with the "Fairness Doctrine." The Progressive Thought Police are the ones behind every attempt to restrict the freedom of speech, to enforce political correctness----but only as means to subverting their political opponents, not as a matter of principle to be equally applied to all. And like all their totalitarian power grabs, they sell them to the public as done in the interest of "equality" and "fairness."

The Progressives want to put everyone on plantations so they can rule over them like feudal lords. Thankfully, they are forced to wait until they can coerce the serfs-to-be to beat their swords into ploughshares. Once they get the guns, all other rights are nullified. Before the Republicans freed the slaves, there was an attempt at arming the blacks and starting an insurrection. This was led by a man named John Brown who clearly understood slavery for what it is: a perpetual state of war waged by slave-owners against the enslaved. As long as Progressives can keep their voters dependent upon the government for their very survival, they can hold onto them as a permanent underclass.

10. Fraudulent Race Cards

The myth that America is a nation of racial bigots competing in a social Darwinist battle for supremacy is propped up by highly charged propaganda which is based upon lies, distortions and outright hoaxes. The Progressive ideology is rooted in narratives, stories, and myths which are reinforced by hoaxes and biased media coverage. For example, Michelle Obama claimed to have been treated like a servant when she went to a Target department store. A much shorter woman asked her to grab a bottle of detergent from the top shelf. Initially, she discussed in incident as a positive interaction. She told David Letterman "I reached up and pulled it down. She said 'Well, you didn't have to make it look so easy.' That was my interaction. I felt so good. She had no idea who I was." Later, when she discussed this incident with People Magazine, she portrayed it as a racial slight, insinuating that she was ignored because she was black, that is, until she was deemed useful for a menial task.

Massachusetts Democratic senator Elizabeth Warren, presumably unfettered by White Guilt, falsely claimed minority status thereby gaining Ivy League tenure. A 1997 Fordham Law Review article refers to her as Harvard Law School's "first woman of color," but today she's better known as "Fauxcahontas."

Racial pandering isn't new in politics.Appealing to stereotypes is how politicians identify with their target demographics. Nobel laureate Toni Morrison famously called Bill Clinton the first "black president", saying, "Clinton displays almost every trope of blackness: single-parent household, born poor, working-class, saxophone-playing, McDonald's-and-junk-food-loving boy from Arkansas." Hillary Clinton even has a "negro dialect" which she employed at a black church in Selma, Alabama. This was not considered offensive because the Clinton's, like wolves in sheep's clothing,posture as friend's of minorities. This also explains why blacks weren't offended when Senator Harry Reid complimented President Obama for not having a "negro dialect".

However, Democrats are by no means the only ones to get into the racial identity group racket. Republican governor Jeb Bush called himself Florida's "first Latino governor" and even marked Hispanic on a 2009 Florida voter registration application. The difference is, the Progressive movement isn't merely pandering for votes. They are using racial politics to segregate and balkanize the United States and disrupt the harmony of a pluralistic,multi-ethnic society. Their objective is to divide and conquer as part of their class warfare agenda.

Every Progressive Identity Group has a built-in need for an oppressor, real or imaginary. Their oppressors are always some form of hater, racist, or phobic. Feminists, in the absence of actual male oppression, grab headlines with false allegations of "campus rape" caused by "rape culture." Even when these hoaxes are exposed, the truth does little to undo the re-enforcement of the fraudulent narratives of the radical Left.

The hoaxes, the lying, and the racial pandering are part of the myth building process. Truth and facts are only applicable insofar as they back up the pre-existing narrative of a deeply troubled, divided nation. This narrative is being demagogued and amplified by the Progressive Media with the expectation that it will become a self-fulfilling prophecy, which it does every time a race riot breaks out over an allegation of "police brutality," another largely mythical construct of the radical Left.

Afterword

The use of the word "pig" as an epithet has long been used by the radical Left to attack the true defenders of American individualism. By taking that word back, we can take back the narrative and ascend the moral high ground from those who would subvert everything that makes America great.

There is power in cultural appropriation and it's time for us to take our power back from the true pigs, the Progressive Identity Groups who are subverting, perverting, and destroying our nation from within.

If you have found this book instructive, please take a look at my author's page at my other publications. Thank you for your time.

---Andrew Coulter